Complete, easy-to-make
Meals made in a Muffin Pan

Muffin *Meals*

Julia Vradelis *and* Allison Worrell

TATE PUBLISHING
AND ENTERPRISES, LLC

Published by Tate Publishing & Enterprises, LLC
127 E. Trade Center Terrace | Mustang, Oklahoma 73064 USA
1.888.361.9473 | www.tatepublishing.com

Tate Publishing is committed to excellence in the publishing industry. The company reflects the philosophy established by the founders, based on Psalm 68:11,
"The Lord gave the word and great was the company of those who published it."

Book design copyright © 2014 by Tate Publishing, LLC. All rights reserved.
Cover and interior design by Errol Villamante
Photos by Julia Vradelis and Allison Worrell, Magan Joplin

Published in the United States of America

ISBN: 978-1-62902-499-8
1. Cooking / Courses & Dishes / General
2. Cooking / General
13.12.18

Dedication

We would like to dedicate this book to the loving memory of Randy and Mona Eckert, Julia's brother and sister-in-law, Mrs. Vera Eckert, Julia's mother and Mrs. Dottie Jane Arnoult, Allison's mother.

Randy and Mona both died of malignant brain tumors within five years of each other. Randy was Julia's oldest brother and was truly a positive influence on everyone he touched. He and Mona would, I'm sure, be supportive of this venture but also laugh at the thought. At one point in their lives, Julia and Randy lived in Houston at the same time. Julia invited her big brother to come over for a "home cooked" meal after work. Long story short…Julia got hung up at work, picked up fast food and slammed it down on the table when she got home. Randy never let her forget it as her attempt at "home cooked".

Julia would also like to dedicate this book to her mother Mrs. Vera Eckert, who is actually a great cook and although currently battling ovarian cancer, continues to stay strong, positive, and is always a source of inspiration.

Authors note:

I am saddened to say, that during the final editing of this book, my Mother, Vera Eckert, lost her battle with ovarian cancer. She did see the proof of the book and was so proud of our efforts. She was also delighted and somewhat surprised at the dedication to her and the credit we gave to her for the original recipe (Sloppy Joe Muffins). My Mom touched so many lives and influenced so many people, with her smile and positive outlook. She supported Allison and me throughout this process with nothing but encouragement and kind words.   I love you and miss you – Julia.

Dottie Jane Arnoult was a wife, mother, grandmother, daughter and sister that impacted so many people's lives. She was originally from eastern North Carolina and eventually returned back there where she joined family to enjoy her well-deserved retirement. That did not last long given her strong drive to stay productive and busy. When Allison started her family, Dottie stepped up as "Nanny" and helped care for Allison's children during the work day. As Allison and Todd's veterinary practice grew, she took on the challenge of part-time office manager, which quickly grew to a full time position as the grandchildren entered school. She was a vital part of the business, and although began with no hands-on veterinary knowledge, her strong business background and willingness to learn allowed her to help manage and guide the business to great success. Many would say it must be difficult to work with your mother, or even more so, your mother-in-law, but Dottie was invaluable. Often, at the end of a long work day she would travel home with Allison for a late afternoon cup of coffee and visit with the little girls she loved so and help catch up household chores. With the loss of her mother, Allison has not only lost her mom, but her coworker and office mate, and as she puts it, her very best friend. Dottie would often tell Allison when times were tough about losing her father to heart disease. She would say,"You really don't know about going through hard times and tragedies until you have experienced the loss of a parent." How true these words have become. Dottie would be very proud of how the family has carried on. It is with fond memories that Allison dedicates this book to Dottie with thanks for being the foundation for all that she has accomplished and all that is yet to come. Allison also thanks her dad, Joe Arnoult, for being there every step of the way.

A portion of the proceeds from this book will be donated to Hospice in their memory and for all those who have lost their lives to cancer.

Acknowledgements

When we started this project, we really had no idea how many people would ultimately be involved in some way. Obviously our families enjoyed the process because they got more home cooked meals than ever before. Not all were good! We appreciate their patience and participation during this process. We also thank our friends who inspired us, cheered us on and offered advice. A special thanks to our contractors down the street (you know who you are) who were our guinea pigs many mornings and continued to test our inventions even after a few flops. Also thank you to the guys at Knuckleheads Bike Shop for being a test market for our muffins. Although we tried to keep the project under wraps for a long time, possibly out of fear of rejection or simply that it was such a great concept that we should be secretive, we did share a few recipes with friends and coworkers that were all eager to try our muffins. Thanks to the girls at PetDocks Veterinary Hospital for the encouragement and to our friends spread across the country that admired photos of our tasty creations. We hope to see you on our book tour! You all kept us going with our eye on the finish line. We would also like to thank one special, kinda smart and witty friend, David, for assisting us with putting our drawings into a printable format for the book. You are the best!

Table of Contents

Introduction

Muffin Meals were created out of a friendship, love, loss, and necessity. Julia Eckert Vradelis and Allison Arnoult Worrell, long-time friends, are both busy moms who don't actually have time, or even like to cook. Enter…Muffin Meals.

In this recipe book, you will find innovative, easy creations that the whole family will enjoy. Muffin Meals are exactly what their name suggests–a meal in the shape of a muffin. They are easy to make, fun to look at, and make great gifts. The portion size is perfect for most individuals, and all of the recipes can be frozen for later.

These Muffin Meals are designed with basic ingredients or prepackaged kits to make preparation both easy and quick. In many cases, as you will see, you can make several different kinds, stick them in the freezer, and you have meals ready for those hectic days when cooking is simply not an option!

Muffin meals make great gifts and are so easy to transport. We have included some fun ways to wrap them up and share as housewarming gifts, bring to a new mom, give to a friend who is under the weather, or just say "I care". We have both suffered losses of loved ones, and one of the things that touched us was the kindness of others who simply brought over a home-cooked meal.

No, we don't love cooking, but we loved making this book. Some of our ideas made us almost "giddy" and others failed miserably, but we enjoyed the process and love the outcome. We truly hope you enjoy it too.

Meet the authors

Julia Eckert Vradelis is not a cook or a writer. But she somehow managed, with her friend Allison, to cook and write. She lives on the coast of North Carolina with her husband and daughters. Julia has a degree in Interior Design from Delta State University. She was a Media Buyer for an advertising agency for many years before becoming the Marketing Director for a privately owned hotel near Cincinnati, Ohio.

Allison Arnoult Worrell lives on the coast of North Carolina with her husband and two daughters. She is a veterinarian and co owner of PetDocks Veterinary Hospital with her husband. She attended the University of Georgia and is still a loyal Bulldog! She loves volunteering at her children's schools, boating, photography, traveling to new places and music.

Welcome to Muffin Meals

You will find in this book, a whole new way of looking at meals. The thing we love about these recipes is that, for the most part, they are quick, easy, yummy, and creative. A few of them will frustrate you until you get the hang of it. But we believe you and your family will enjoy making and eating them.

Muffin Meals are easy to make, easy to clean up, and easy to give as gifts. They also freeze well, so spend a Sunday afternoon making several batches and you will have dinner during the week with the press of a microwave button.

Mix and Match

When we were kids, our Moms made one meal. We ate that meal or we went hungry. Now, we seem to be making several different meals. No need to get in to the reasoning why. It just happens. Muffin Meals are the perfect solution. You can mix and match recipes to suit the taste of everyone in your family. Make 2 Shepherd's Pies and 4 Meatloaves. Use your cooked and shredded chicken for 3 Chicken Enchilada Meals and 3 Chicken Parmesan Meals. Simply adjust the recipes to suit your tastes. The Pizza Muffins and Sandwich Stackers can all be "made to order" and you can involve your children in making them.

You can also experiment with the breads. In the recipes calling for the "cup" to be made out of bread, you can use crescent roll dough, biscuit dough, pizza dough or French bread dough. It really just depends on your preference.

Mix to Muffin Cup

"Mix to Muffin Cup" will be noted under the title of the Muffin Meals that are very easy and very fast to make, since you start with a kit. Just remember to have the ingredients on hand for that mix. If you need a quick dinner, these would be the ones to look for!

Portion Control

You will notice that in this book we did not include a calorie count. We plan to produce a "Lean Muffin Meals" book, however, for this one we just wanted to start a concept and create delicious meals that are fun and easy to make. There is also something to be said for "portion control". By making these in single portion sizes, you really have to choose to have that second one (and in some cases, that's perfectly fine). But it's much easier to take several spoonfuls of casserole, for instance, and still call it a single serving, verses sticking to one "Muffin Meal". One of our favorite products is the giant wine glass that holds an entire bottle of wine. You can say you're only having one glass, but let's face it, that one glass is going to get you pretty tipsy!

Do you know the Muffin Pan?

There are a few pointers to getting started. First, you need some muffin pans. Surprisingly, there are many different types, styles and brands. Most of the recipes in this book use the large or "Texas Style" muffin pans. The sandwich recipes work best with the smaller, straight cup pan. Many of the desserts are made in the regular size pans simply because they are not meant to be entire meals. This is not to say that everyone shouldn't have dessert for a meal every once in a while. Life is short, right?

The Must-Have

Muffin Pans – We just covered this. Kind of a no-brainer.

Non-stick cooking spray – You will use this in almost every recipe. What did we do without it?

Muffin Pulls – (patent pending) Hopefully by the time you are reading this you can purchase these online. You can also make these fairly easily by folding tin foil to form strips about 6" long and 3/4" wide. Remember to spray non-stick cooking spray (when the recipe calls for it) after you insert these in the muffin cups. If there is too much excess in the regular size muffin tins, simply roll or fold edges to adjust.

Foil Balls – These will be used in a number of recipes to keep the outer shell from falling in on itself. Please remember to spray the bottom half of these before placing in the "shells" so they don't stick!

Parchment Paper – We use this for a number of different uses. Please refer to "quotes" at the back of the book regarding this one.

Mani Pedi's – Mainly we just wanted to see if you were paying attention. But you will have time to pamper yourself because you won't be stuck in the kitchen all day!

"I always cook with wine. Sometimes I even add it to the food"

--W.C. Fields

Beef Muffin
Meals

Beef Burgundy Bowls

Makes 6 large Muffin Meals

6 Woven Bread Bowls (See "How To" section)
1 1/2 - 2 lbs. beef stew meat
1 tsp. garlic
Olive Oil
1 can beef broth
1 cup red wine (you can substitute cooking sherry)
1 small carton of button mushrooms, rinsed and halved
1 small package of pearl onions, peeled
3/4 cup instant brown rice
Sour Cream
French fried Onion rings for garnish

Brown beef in skillet in olive oil. Add garlic. Remove from skillet and add to either crock pot or large pot on the stove. Add beef broth and next 3 ingredients. (If you are using red wine, pour a glass and enjoy. It's 5 o'clock somewhere!) Bring to a boil (on the stove top) then reduce heat to simmer, or set on high in the crock pot for 2 hours. Add rice and cook an additional 15 to 30 minutes or until rice is tender. Serve in bread bowls. Garnish with a dollop of sour cream and French fried onion rings. Need we say it? Enjoy with another glass of wine. You deserve it!

Julia Vradelis and Allison Worrell

California Sun-dried Tomato & Beef Cups

Makes 6 large Muffin Meals

1 lb. ground beef, browned and drained
1 can beef broth
1 8.5 oz. jar of sun-dried tomatoes in oil
1/2 cup pine nuts, lightly toasted
1/4 cup grated parmesan cheese
4 1/2 cups dry extra broad ribbon noodles
1/2 cup shredded mozzarella cheese
1/2 tsp. garlic powder
1/2 tsp. salt
1 jar of your favorite spaghetti sauce

Preheat oven to 350 degrees. Place Muffin Pulls in muffin cups, and spray with non-stick cooking spray. Combine beef broth, tomatoes, and pine nuts in a blender. Blend until smooth. Add this mixture to the browned ground beef. Add parmesan cheese and set aside. No need to heat this mixture. Cook noodles according to directions. After draining the noodles, stir in mozzarella cheese, salt, garlic powder and let sit for about 5 minutes. This will make the noodles sticky and easier to shape. Put about 3/4 cup in each muffin cup and press with a spoon to form a "cup". This is sometimes easier to do with your fingers. It will not be perfect, but make a "middle" to put the meat mixture in. Add a generous amount of the meat mixture in each cup. Press down as you go. You will have some left over. Just freeze it for another day or you can double the noodles and make 12! Bake for 10-20 minutes. Remove from oven and let sit for about 10

Julia Vradelis and Allison Worrell

minutes. This is important because the noodles will fall apart if you try to take them out of the muffin cups immediately. After you plate these, you can serve with heated spaghetti sauce on the side or drizzled on top. Top with additional mozzarella cheese.

Down and Dirty Rice Muffins

Makes 6 large Muffin Meals

Mix to Muffin version:
Simply pick up a Dirty Rice Mix (we love Zatarains) and skip right to the crescent roll step.

1 lb. ground beef, browned
2 cups cooked rice
1/2 cup minced onion
1/2 cup chopped green pepper
1/2 cup chopped red pepper
1 T. chili powder
1/2 tsp. cumin
1 tsp. garlic powder
1/2 tsp. salt
2 cans crescent rolls
   or 1 can thin pizza crust dough

Preheat oven to 350 degrees. Insert Muffin Pulls into muffin cups and spray with non-stick cooking spray.

Combine first 9 ingredients. Spread out dough on parchment paper or pastry cloth. If you are using crescent dough, you will want to seal the perforated edges together. Cut dough in to 5" squares and place in large muffin cups. Fill with dirty rice mixture, leaving enough room to gather the four corners to meet in the center. .

Bake for 15 minutes or until dough is golden brown. Remove from pan. For and extra "kick" top with hot sauce or chili sauce.

Creative touch: These already look like "presents" and will travel well. Put these on some fun New Orleans scrapbook paper and include a small bottle of hot sauce for a special touch.

Julia Vradelis and Allison Worrell

Impossibly Good Cheeseburger Muffins

Makes 6 large Muffin Meals or 12 regular Muffin Meals

1 lb. ground beef
1/2 cup chopped onion
1/2 tsp. salt
1/4 tsp. pepper
1 cup shredded cheddar cheese
1 1/2 cups milk
3/4 cup Bisquick
3 eggs

Preheat oven to 350 degrees. Insert Muffin Pulls and lightly spray muffin pan with non-stick cooking spray. Brown ground beef with chopped onion and drain. Stir in salt and pepper. Divide evenly among muffin cups. Sprinkle with cheddar cheese. Beat remaining ingredients until smooth. Pour evenly over muffin cups. Bake until brown or until knife comes out clean. Approximately 25 minutes. This freezes well.

Julia Vradelis and Allison Worrell

Lasagna Roll Ups

Makes 6 large Muffin Meals

1 ½ lbs. of ground beef browned and drained
1 jar Spaghetti Sauce
1 jar Alfredo Sauce
1 cup chopped spinach, fresh or frozen thawed
1 8 oz. package of shredded mozzarella cheese
Garlic powder
Oregano
Salt and pepper
6 Precooked Lasagna noodles (You may want to cook a few extra in case one tears)

Preheat oven to 350 degrees. Put Muffin Pulls in large muffin cups and spray with non-stick cooking spray. Assemble all the ingredients. Lay out parchment paper or wax paper to lay out the noodles. Layer a thin layer of spaghetti sauce, ground beef, spinach, alfredo sauce, and cheese. Sprinkle with garlic, oregano, salt and pepper. Carefully roll up noodles. It will be messy, and some ingredients will probably fall out, but the end result is beautiful! Place each roll up in the muffin cup, top with additional sauce and bake for 10 minutes or until cheese is bubbly.

Let them rest for 5 min. before removing from pan. Serve with heated spaghetti sauce or alfredo sauce and cheese.

Julia Vradelis and Allison Worrell

Layer ingredients on lasagna noodles.

After you place the roll ups in the pan, spoon sauce over the top.

Top with additional sauce and cheese and dive in!

Note: If you plan to transport these, you may want to reinforce with a toothpick. Just make sure the recipient knows they're there!!

Meatloaf Muffins

Makes 12 regular Muffin Meals

1 1/2 lbs. ground beef
1 cup plain bread crumbs
1 tsp. salt
1 tsp. garlic powder
3 T. minced onion
1 egg
1/2 tsp. ground yellow mustard
1/2 tsp. ground red pepper
1/4 tsp. black pepper

Topping:
1 cup ketchup
1 T. Brown Sugar
1 T. White Vinegar
1 tsp. ground yellow mustard

Preheat oven to 350 degrees. Insert Muffin Pulls. (No need to grease pans.) Combine all ingredients and press in to regular muffin cups. Bake 15-20 minutes or until browned all the way through. While the meatloaves are baking, mix up ingredients for topping. Set aside. Take a paper towel and blot the grease from each meatloaf. Top each meatloaf with 1-2 T. of topping. Bake an additional 5 minutes. Let rest for 5 minutes. Remove from pan and serve with a salad or side vegetable. Just like Mom used to make! Literally!

Now I know that you would assume we would just say "top with your favorite barbecue sauce" which you could but this was a staple at our house and that simple recipe of my Mom's was so good, we insist you make it. Here's to Vera!

Shepherd's Pie Muffin Meals

Makes 6 large Muffin Meals

A classic with a twist… Shepherd's pie meal muffins are a meat and potatoes staple with minimal prep time and maximum flavor!

   1 lb. of ground beef
   1 package of onion soup mix
   2 cups mashed potatoes
   1 cup shredded carrots
   1 1/2 cups of green peas
   1 cup shredded cheddar cheese

Preheat oven to 350 degrees. Place Muffin Pulls in large muffin cups. No need to coat with non-stick spray. Mix together ground beef and onion soup mix. Fill muffin cups 2/3 full. Indent the center to be filled later. Bake at 350° for 20 min. or until center is no longer pink. Drain grease (we simply blot with paper towels). Divide carrots and peas evenly in to ground beef shells. Top with mashed potatoes and bake an additional 10 min. Top with shredded cheddar cheese. Enjoy!

Julia Vradelis and Allison Worrell

Spaghetti Muffin Meals

Makes 6 large Muffin Meals

1 lb. of ground beef
1 tsp. of garlic salt
1 T. melted butter
1 tsp. oregano
1/2 tsp. of salt-and-pepper
1 jar of spaghetti sauce
1 roll of refrigerated French bread
2 cups of angel hair pasta, cooked
Parmesan cheese
Shredded mozzarella

Preheat oven to 350 degrees. Insert Muffin Pulls and spray with non-stick cooking spray. Brown ground beef. Add salt, pepper, and oregano. Drain and add spaghetti sauce and cooked spaghetti. Continue to simmer on low. Rollout French bread dough and cut in 4 inch circles-a bowl or saucepan cover can be used to cut out circles. Place in muffin cups and spread to cover up the sides. Brush bread dough with melted butter and sprinkle with garlic salt. Bake bread 10 min. at 350°. Remove from oven and fill with spaghetti mixture. Sprinkle with Parmesan cheese and bake an additional 10 min. Top with mozzarella.

Julia Vradelis and Allison Worrell

Creative touch: If you're bringing these to someone special, put them in a large cupcake box (you can find these at your local craft store). Line the bottom of the box with red and white checked scrapbook paper and put a small glass votive candle in the middle. Voila! Grab a bottle of wine and you have provided a lovely Italian setting for dinner.

Sweet and Sour Porcupines

Makes 6 large Muffin Meals

Porcupine cups:
- 1 1/2 lbs. of ground beef
- 1/2 cup instant rice (brown or white)
- 1/2 cup water
- 2 T. minced onion
- 1 egg
- 1 tsp. salt
- 1/2 tsp. celery seed
- 1/2 tsp. garlic powder
- 1/8 tsp. pepper

Sweet and Sour Veggies:
- 1/2 cup brown sugar
- 1 T. cornstarch
- 1 can (13 oz.) pineapple tidbits
- 1/2 cup vinegar
- 1 T. soy sauce
- 1 green pepper, coarsely chopped

Preheat Oven to 350 degrees. Insert Muffin Pulls. Do not spray with non-stick spray. Mix all ingredients for meat mixture. Put approximately 1/2 cup of mixture in large muffin cups. With a spoon, press down in the middle to form a cup. Mixture should come up to the top of the cup but not spill over. Bake 15 minutes or until brown. Take a paper towel and absorb the grease from each cup.

While the "cups" are baking, mix brown sugar and cornstarch in a medium skillet. Add pineapple (with syrup), vinegar, and soy sauce. Add green pepper and heat to boiling, stirring constantly. Reduce heat, cover and simmer for 10 minutes.

Remove cups from the muffin tins and top with veggies and sauce. Enjoy.

Julia Vradelis and Allison Worrell

Taco Muffin Meals

"Mix to Muffin Cup"

Makes 6 large Muffin Meals

1 box of Jiffy cornbread mix (and ingredients according to package)
1 lb. ground beef
1 package taco seasoning
Taco sauce

Toppings:

Shredded cheddar cheese
Shredded lettuce
Sour cream
Jalapeños

Preheat oven to 350°. Insert Muffin Pulls and spray with non-stick cooking spray. Prepare cornbread according to package. Leave in bowl and set aside. Brown ground beef and drain grease thoroughly. Add taco seasoning and 1/4 cup of water to beef. Fill each muffin pan with 1/4 cup of cornmeal batter. Add meat mixture and 1 tablespoon taco sauce. Top with remaining batter and bake for 20 minutes. Let rest for 5 minutes before removing from pan by gently pulling Muffin Pulls. Top with cheese, lettuce, sour cream, and jalapeños.

Creative touch: serve these on small terra-cotta saucers that you can find at the local gardening store. Drizzle plate with taco sauce or for a bigger "kick", habanero sauce!

"All you have to do is hold the chicken, bring me the toast, give me a check for the chicken salad sandwich and you haven't broken any rules"

Jack Nicholson in 'Five Easy Pieces'(1970)

Chicken Muffin
Meals

Chicken and Spinach Dip Muffins

"Mix to Muffin Cup"

Makes 6 large Muffin Meals

1 Knorr's Dry Vegetable Soup Mix
1 package frozen chopped spinach, thawed and drained
1 can water chestnuts, drained and minced
1 cup Miracle Whip Salad Dressing
1 cup sour cream
2 cups cooked chicken, chopped
1 package refrigerated Phyllo dough

This recipe follows the one printed on the package of soup mix for spinach dip. We have simply added chicken.

Preheat oven to 350 degrees. Insert Muffin Pulls in to each muffin cup and spray with non-stick cooking spray.

Combine all ingredients (except dough). Spread out phyllo dough on parchment paper. Cut into 6 squares and follow directions in the "How To" section for making Phyllo Cups.

Fill each phyllo cup with chicken and spinach mixture. Bake for 10-12 minutes or until dough is golden brown.

Let cool for 5 minutes. Remove and serve!

Julia Vradelis and Allison Worrell

Chicken Caprese Muffins

Makes 6 large Muffin Meals

2 cups chopped cooked chicken
1 cup Italian bread crumbs
1/4 tsp. salt
1/4 tsp. black pepper
3 T olive oil
1/4 cup lemon juice
1 egg beaten
1 tsp. dried basil
1/2 cup feta cheese crumbled
1/2 cup tomato basil cream sauce

Preheat oven to 350°. Insert Muffin Pulls into large muffin cups. Spray with non-stick cooking spray. Mix all of the ingredients and fill all 6 muffin cups evenly. Bake for 15 minutes. While muffins are cooking, make the tomato basil cream sauce (see recipe below). Remove muffins from oven and let rest for about 5 min. Remove from pan and serve with tomato basil cream sauce. Top with additional feta cheese, fresh basil, and a lemon wedge.

Tomato basil cream sauce

1 1/2 cups spaghetti sauce (basil and tomato is our pick!)
3 T heavy cream
1 tsp. dried basil

Combine ingredients and cook over low heat in saucepan. Stir constantly. Pour 2 to 3 tablespoons over each muffin. You'll want to lick the spoon every time (but wait till you serve everyone!)

Julia Vradelis and Allison Worrell

Chicken Cordon Bleu Muffins

Makes 4 to 6 large Muffin Meals

1 can of refrigerated bread or crescent rolls
3 boneless, skinless, thin-sliced chicken breasts – cut into 2 inch squares
Thin slices of ham, cut into 2 inch squares
3 slices of Swiss cheese, yep 2 inch squares
1 jar of sundried tomatoes
1 can of Cream of Mushroom Soup
1/2 cup sour cream
1/2 cup of white wine or cooking sherry

Mix together soup, sour cream and wine. Set aside.

Preheat oven to 350 degrees. If you are using crescent rolls for this recipe, it will make 4 muffins. For testing purposes, we used the whole wheat bread loaf dough and it makes 6 large muffins. Spray muffin tins with non-stick cooking spray. Place dough (cut into squares) in the muffins tins with corners of dough coming out of cups. We suggest assembling these one at a time since the dough overlaps each cup until you add the filling. In the bottom of each cup, layer ham, cheese and chicken. Top with another layer of ham and cheese and finally 1 T. chopped sundried tomatoes. Finally, add 1 T. of soup mixture. Fold the corners of dough together forming a "bow" at the top.

Bake for 20 minutes. While these are baking, heat up the remaining sauce. Remove from tins and serve with sauce. Tres Bon!

Julia Vradelis and Allison Worrell

Chicken Enchiladas

Makes 6 large Muffin Meals

2 cups chopped cooked chicken
1 can condensed cream of chicken soup
8 flour tortillas (6 inch)
1 can (14-1/2 oz.) Mexican-flavored diced tomatoes, undrained
1 cup Mexican Style Shredded Cheese
1/2 can sliced black olives
Sour cream
Pico de gallo

Heat oven to 350°F. Place tortillas in muffin pan. (Refer to "How To" section for this.) Combine chicken and soup; Spoon chicken mixture into tortillas. Mix tomatoes, shredded cheese and black olives and spoon over chicken.

Top with a sprinkle of cheese.

Cover with foil.

Bake 30 to 35 min. or until cheese is melted and chicken is heated through, removing foil after 20 min.

Top with sour cream, guacamole and pico de gallo and enjoy!

Julia Vradelis and Allison Worrell

Feel free to spice this one up with green chilies or jalapenos.

Chicken Fajita Muffins

Makes 8 large Muffin Meals

1 package of chicken tenderloin strips
1 yellow pepper
1 green pepper
1 red onion
1 bottle Allegro original marinade
8 flour tortillas

Preheat oven to 350 degrees. Place tortillas in muffin cups (refer to "How to" section). Chop the onion and peppers in bite size pieces. Wash and cut the chicken into cubes. Place the chicken, peppers and onion in a skillet and stir fry with the allegro marinade until chicken is fully cooked. Spoon the fajita mixture into the tortillas in the muffin pan. Bake approximately 10-15 minutes. Remove and serve with favorite fajita toppings such as sour cream or guacamole. To ensure the chicken mixture does not dry out while baking, the tortillas may be baked alone with foil balls inserted as space savers and then filled with fajita mixture to serve.

Chicken Parmesan Muffins

Makes 6 large Muffin Meals

3 chicken breasts, cooked and shredded
1 jar marinara sauce (reserve 1 cup)
One half loaf of Italian bread, torn in small pieces
1 bag shredded mozzarella cheese (put 1/2 bag in mixture, reserve the rest for topping)
3/4 cup Parmesan cheese
1 teaspoon oregano
1 teaspoon garlic salt

Preheat oven to 350°. Spray non-stick cooking spray in each muffin cup. Mix all the ingredients in a large bowl. Fill each muffin cup with mixture (fill all the way to the top). Bake for 15 min. Remove from oven and let stand for 10 min. before removing from pans. Top with remaining marinara (2 tablespoons per muffin). Top with mozzarella cheese and fresh oregano leaves.

Julia Vradelis and Allison Worrell

Chicken Roll Ups

Makes 6-8 large Muffin Meals

1 pkg boneless skinless chicken tenderloins
1-8 oz.package of cream cheese
1 box frozen spinach thawed and drained
Dash of garlic
Dash cayenne pepper
Dash of nutmeg
Dash of salt and Pepper
1 box ready cooked bacon
1 can Swanson's chicken broth

Preheat oven to 350 degrees. Pound out the chicken on wax paper until thin. Mix the cream cheese, the spinach and the spices in a bowl. Spread some of the mixture on each piece of chicken. Roll up the strip and wrap with bacon. Place in the muffin cups. Pour a tablespoon or two of chicken broth over each chicken roll up. Bake until bacon is crisp, about 30-40 minutes.

Julia Vradelis and Allison Worrell

Chicken Pot Pie Muffins

Makes 6 large Muffin Meals

Refrigerated pie crust dough
3 chicken breasts, cooked and shredded
1 can cream of chicken soup
2 stalks of celery
1 cup shredded carrots
1 cup of cooked peas
1/2 cup instant mashed potato flakes
Salt and pepper to taste

Preheat oven to 350°. Insert Muffin Pulls and spray cups with non-stick cooking spray. Spread out pie crust dough and cut into 6 inch circles (you can use a lid for this or trace around a saucer or bowl) (refer to "How-To" section). Fill each cup with the dough and shape around the sides. Crimp the edges as you would with a standard pie crust. In small pan, sauté celery and carrots and 1 tablespoon olive oil until tender. Combine chicken and next 5 ingredients. Add salt and pepper. Fill each muffin cup with mixture and bake for 15 min.

Put a fun Fall twist on this. See "Holiday" section

Good Ole Chicken and Rice Cups

"Mix to Muffin Cup"

Makes 6 large Muffin Meals

Cornbread Stuffing Mix
Chicken Flavored Rice Mix
3 Chicken Breasts, cooked and diced
1/2 cup chopped fresh parsley
1 red, yellow, and orange bell pepper, diced
1/2 can Cream of Chicken Soup

Preheat oven to 350 degrees. Place Muffin Pulls in large muffin cups and spray with non-stick cooking spray. In a large bowl, mix 2 cups stuffing mix with 1 cup water. Put 1/3 of cornbread mixture in to each muffin cup and shape in to a cup. (Refer to "How To" section. This is the same concept as the rice cups) Bake for 20 minutes. Meanwhile, prepare rice according to directions. Add remaining ingredients. After cups have baked, remove from oven and fill generously with rice mixture. Bake an additional 10-15 minutes or until heated through.

Remove from oven. Let rest 5 minutes before removing from pan. Top with slices of bell pepper or remaining soup heated up and a fresh parsley sprig.

Mexican Chicken and Corn Muffins

Makes 6 large Muffin Meals

6 corn tortillas
2 cups cooked chicken, diced
1 box frozen corn soufflé
1 can corn
1 red pepper diced
1 envelope taco seasoning
Shredded cheddar cheese
Sour cream and jalapeño slices

Preheat oven to 350°. Spray muffin cups with non-stick cooking spray. Place one tortilla in each muffin cup (you will have to fold to fit – see under "How-To" section). Combine next 5 ingredients and 1/4 cup of cheese. Stuff tortilla shells with mixture and bake for 10 min. Top with cheese, sour cream, and jalapeño slice.

Julia Vradelis and Allison Worrell

"I will not eat oysters. I want my food dead. Not sick. Not wounded. Dead."

Woody Allen

Seafood Muffin

Meals

Caribbean Shrimp Muffins

Makes 6 large Muffin Meals

1 package Caribbean rice mix (Zatarian's was used for this recipe)
24 fresh or frozen shrimp, peeled and deveined
1 can coconut milk
1 can chopped pineapple, reserving 2 tablespoons juice
1 Ripe Mango, chopped
1 jalapeño, minced
Olive oil

Preheat oven to 350°. Insert Muffin Pulls and spray cups with non-stick cooking spray. Prepare rice according to directions. Put 1/2 cup of cooked rice in each muffin cup. Press down the center with a spoon to form a "cup" (refer to "How To" section). Bake 10 minutes. Remove from oven. While rice cups are in oven, stir-fry shrimp in 2 tablespoons olive oil until pink, 5 to 10 minutes. Add coconut milk and simmer on low for an additional 10 minutes. Mix chopped pineapple with 2 tablespoons of pineapple juice and chopped mango. Add minced jalapeño. Carefully pull rice cups from muffin pan by lifting Muffin Pulls. Put 3 to 4 coconut shrimp in each rice cup and top with mango salsa mixture.

Delicious Mon!

Creative touch: If you are transporting these, we highly recommend wrapping with decorative cup wrappers (pattern is in back of book). Tie wrappers with raffia to continue the island theme. Serve the Pineapple and Mango salsa in a hollowed out pineapple shell and let people help themselves.

Julia Vradelis and Allison Worrell

Shrimp and Grits Muffins

Makes 6 large Muffin Meals

1 pound of fresh shrimp
1 cup barbecue sauce
Instant grits
2/3 cup shredded cheddar cheese
1/2 cup green onions, diced
1/2 tsp. garlic
1 tsp. salt
Bacon bits

Preheat oven to 350 degrees. Insert Muffin Pulls and spray with non-stick cooking spray. Shell, devein, and remove tails of shrimp. Sauté shrimp in olive oil over medium heat. Cook about 5 to 7 min. until shrimp turn pink. Add barbecue sauce, cover and simmer on low. Cook grits for 4 servings according to package (this will make 6 muffin meals). Add cheese, onions, garlic, salt, and bacon bits. Insert Muffin Pulls in your muffin pans. Spray with non-stick cooking spray thoroughly. Fill muffin cup 1/2 full with grits. Bake in the oven for 15 min. or until set. Remove from oven and let sit for 5 min. Carefully, lift out of the muffin cups and set on a plate. Top with 3 to 4 shrimp on each one. Serve with your favorite cole slaw.

Creative touch: Serve or deliver these on a round platter lined with a green leafy lettuce. In the center, have a bowl with the barbecue shrimp so people can serve themselves.

Crab and Pasta Muffins

Makes 6 large Muffin Meals

1 small can of flaked crabmeat
Sun-dried tomatoes in oil (diced)
2 cups baby spinach leaves
1 package wide pasta noodles
Salt and pepper
Aioli sauce

Preheat oven to 350°. Insert Muffin Pulls and spray with non-stick cooking spray. Boil 1/2 bag of noodles according to directions. Drain water but do not rinse, leaving noodles somewhat sticky. Add salt and pepper to taste. Place about 1/2 cup of cooked noodles in each cup and pressed down with the back of a spoon to form a cup in the center of each. Meanwhile, sauté spinach and diced sun-dried tomatoes (use some of the oil from the tomatoes for extra flavor) until spinach is wilted. Put one spoonful of spinach mixture on top of noodles in each cup. Top with one spoonful of crabmeat. Bake for 10 min. Let sit for 5 min. Gently remove from pan and drizzle with aioli sauce.

Creative touch: Remove the top tip from the crabmeat can so there are no sharp edges. Wash can thoroughly and dry. Pour the aioli sauce in that to serve.

Julia Vradelis and Allison Worrell

Crab Cake Muffins

Makes 6 large Muffin Meals

1 lb. Lump Crabmeat, cooked
½ cup plain bread crumbs
1 egg
½ cup mayonnaise
1 tsp. Worcestershire
1 tsp. Dijon Mustard
1 tsp. red pepper
1 T. minced onion

Preheat oven to 350 degrees. Insert Muffin Pulls and spray with non-stick cooking spray.

Combine all ingredients, folding in crabmeat last. Bake for 15 minutes. Let cool for 5 minutes then remove from pan and enjoy!

Serve with your preference of cocktail sauce, tartar sauce, or our favorite – a spicy aioli sauce.

Creative touch: Yes. Clearly we do not want you to throw that crabmeat can away. So, you guessed it, remove lip, wash, dry and serve a side of cole slaw in it! (We're gonna keep mentioning this idea until you do it.)

Fish & Chip Cups

Makes 6 large Muffin Meals

3 cups refrigerated hash browns
18 frozen popcorn fish nuggets
3 slices American cheese
Salt and pepper
Tartar sauce

Preheat oven to 375 degrees. Insert Muffin Pulls and spray with non-stick cooking spray. Put 1/2 cup of hash browns in each muffin cup. Using the back of a spoon, press hash browns to form a cup. Sprinkle with salt and pepper. Place 1/4 of a slice of cheese in the bottom of the "cup". Place 3 popcorn fish nuggets in each cup. Bake for 15-20 minutes or until the hash browns are golden brown. Place another 1/4 slice of cheese on top of each cup and bake another 1-2 minutes until cheese melts. Remove from oven and let rest for 2-3 minutes. Remove from pan and serve with tartar sauce. A new twist on a British classic!

Creative Touch: Set your table like a British Pub – with butcher paper and give everyone a marker to draw on it while they eat. Don't forget to add a pint of your favorite brew!

Jambalaya Muffins
"Mix to Muffin Cup"
Makes 6 large Muffin Meals

1 Jiffy Corn Bread Mix
1 pkg. Jambalaya Mix
1/2 lb. fresh or frozen shrimp, shelled, deveined and cut into thirds
Hot Sauce

Preheat oven to 350 degrees. Insert Muffin Pulls and spray non-stick cooking spray. Prepare Jambalaya according to package. Add shrimp to Jambalaya mixture. Prepare Corn Bread Mix according to package. Spoon 1/4 cup of cornbread batter in each muffin cup. Add 2 heaping spoonfuls of Jambalaya Mix to each cup. Top with enough Cornbread batter to cover Jambalaya mixture. Bake for 15 minutes or until cornbread is golden. Top with more Jambalaya and serve.

This recipe can also be made with beef smokies or chicken.

Heat things up by drizzling with your favorite hot sauce!

Creative touch: These are a great way to celebrate Fat Tuesday! Using the wrapper pattern in the back of the book, cover each muffin with festive Mardi Gras papers and lay multicolored bead necklaces around them on the tray. Serve with a "Hurricane" and you have a party New Orleans style!

Julia Vradelis and Allison Worrell

Salmon and Crab Roll ups

Makes 12 regular size Muffin Meals

6 Salmon filets (1/4" thick) (We bought three filets and sliced them thinner to make six)
1/2 cup lump crabmeat (fresh)
Shredded carrots
1/4 cup fresh dill
4 oz. cream cheese
1 egg beaten
1 cup Panko bread crumbs
Salt and pepper
Green onions
1 lemon or lemon juice

Preheat oven to 350 degrees. Insert 1 muffin pull in each muffin cup and spray with non-stick cooking spray. Lay out filets on cutting board (or we use parchment paper for easy clean up). Salt and pepper each filet. Mix cream cheese and dill. Spread evenly on each filet (do this carefully as filets are easy to tear). At one end of filet, place approximately 1 T. of crabmeat and carrots. Begin rolling up from that end. Roll fairly tightly so it stays together. While holding the roll together, brush with beaten egg and sprinkle bottom 3/4 of roll up with bread crumbs. Carefully pull off a strand from the green onions and carefully tie around each roll up. (These can break so be gentle. Just tie once – no need to "knot" it) Place in muffin cup and repeat with remaining filets. Bake for 20 minutes. Let rest for 5 minutes. Sprinkle with lemon juice and enjoy!

Julia Vradelis and Allison Worrell

Creative touch: Remove sharp lip from around the top of the crabmeat can. Wash thoroughly and dry. Cut extra lemons wedges and place in the can for people who want to squeeze a little extra lemon! (Told you we wouldn't let this go!)

Tuna Mac-N-Cheese Muffins

Makes 6 large Muffin Meals

1 box Kraft macaroni and cheese
2 pouches (or cans) of tuna
1/2 cup chopped celery
1/4 cup sweet pickle relish
1/2 cup Miracle Whip salad dressing

Make macaroni and cheese according to directions. Set aside.

Preheat oven to 350°. Insert Muffin Pulls into muffin cups and spray with non-stick cooking spray. Fill each muffin cup with enough macaroni to cover bottom and sides of cups (use the back of a spoon to press the macaroni into a "cup" shape). Combine tuna with remaining ingredients. Fill each cup with tuna mixture and bake for 10 to 12 min. or until tuna is heated through.

Yum! This is the ultimate in comfort food!

Tuna Casserole Muffins

"Mix to Muffin Cups"

Makes 6 large Muffin Meals

2 cans croissant rolls
1 tuna helper box mix
Ingredients for Tuna Helper
1 can mixed vegetables

Preheat oven to 350 degrees. Spray muffin pan with non-stick spray. Unroll croissant rolls and cut in squares. Do not tear along perforations. cut dough into 8 equal squares. Place one square in muffin pan and then layer another on top of it at an angle. (You will have squares left over. If you have two large muffin pans, go ahead and make the extra. Or just roll up and bake as a crescent roll.)

Prepare tuna casserole according to instructions for mix. Add 1 can mixed vegetables drained. Spoon mixture into muffin cups. Bake for 11-13 minutes or until bread shell is golden brown. Allow to cool in the muffin pan 5-10 minutes before serving.

Julia Vradelis and Allison Worrell

"Sandwiches are wonderful. You don't need a spoon or a plate."

--Paul Lynde

Sandwich Muffin
Meals

Buffalo Chicken Wing Muffins

Makes 8 regular Muffin Meals or 16 Mini Muffin Snacks

1 package of chicken tenderloin strips
1 jar buffalo wing sauce-your favorite
1 bottle blue cheese dressing
2-3 stalks celery
2 cups sharp cheddar cheese
1 can regular size biscuits

Preheat oven according to instructions for biscuits. Bring to boil a large pot of water. Cut chicken tenders into cubes. Place chicken in boiling water until cooked then drain and rinse. Place chicken in a mixing bowl. Next add 1 cup blue cheese dressing, 1/2 cup wing sauce, 1/4 cup diced celery (optional), 2 cups cheddar cheese and mix.

If using biscuits to make mini muffins, separate 1 biscuit in half and place 1/2 biscuit in a muffin cup. Place a spoonful of chicken stuffing in center of biscuit. Then press edges together around the filling. Follow with the other half of the biscuit which makes another muffin Repeat until all muffin cups are full. If making regular size muffins, place 1 biscuit in each muffin cup. Spoon 1 T. of chicken mixture on biscuit and press down until biscuit caves in. Pinch sides of biscuit together surrounding, chicken filling.

Bake according to biscuit packaging or until golden brown. Top with more cheese, celery or blue cheese dressing if desired and serve.

Julia Vradelis and Allison Worrell

Chicken Gyros

Makes 6 large Muffin Meals

1 lb. boneless skinless chicken breasts cut in to small pieces
4 T. Olive Oil
1/3 cup lemon juice
1/2 tsp. garlic
1/2 tsp. ground mustard
1 tsp. oregano

1/2 cup peeled chopped cucumber
1/2 cup plain yogurt
1 T. Dill weed
Small red onion
Refrigerated can of thin pizza crust dough

In a large zip lock bag, place chicken, olive oil, lemon juice, garlic, mustard, and oregano. Shake to coat the chicken. Let this marinade for several hours in refrigerator.

Combine cucumber, yogurt, and dill weed and refrigerate.

Preheat oven to 350 degrees. Spray large muffin pan with non-stick cooking spray. Unroll pizza dough and cut into 6 squares. Place each square in to muffin cups. (four corners of dough should be coming out of cup slightly) To keep the shape, insert balls of tin foil – making sure to spray dough with cooking spray or drizzle olive oil to keep the foil from sticking. Bake for 15-20 minutes or until dough is golden.

Julia Vradelis and Allison Worrell

While the "shells" are baking, drain the marinade from the chicken mixture and discard. Sauté chicken for approximately 10 minutes or until juices run clear.

Fill each bread shell with chicken, drizzle with yogurt dressing, and top with thinly sliced red onion. Add a kalamato olive for the final touch.

Greek Pizza Muffins

Makes 8 large Muffin Meals

Crumbled feta cheese
Kalamato or black olives
Purple onions (diced)
Sliced cherry tomatoes
Baby spinach leaves
Can of biscuit dough
Garlic powder
Olive oil

Preheat oven to 350°. Insert Muffin Pulls into muffin cups and spray with non-stick cooking spray. Put one biscuit in each cup and work up the sides of the cup. Sprinkle with olive oil and a dash of garlic powder. Layer the top 5 ingredients until the cup is full. Bake for 15 min. Remove from oven and serve!

Side suggestion: to complete the theme, serve with a Greek salad and a light white wine such as a Pinot Grigio or if you like, ouzo!

Creative touch – print out a copy of the Greek flag and put it on a toothpick to top off your muffins. Opa!

Julia Vradelis and Allison Worrell

Reuben Sandwich Muffins

Makes 4 large Muffin Meals

1 can of crescent rolls or one can of whole wheat bread dough
1 package corned beef sandwich slices
Thousand Island dressing
Swiss cheese
One can sauerkraut

Preheat oven to 350°. Insert Muffin Pulls and spray muffin cups with non-stick cooking spray. Line each cup with 2 overlapping triangles of crescent roll dough or a 5" square of bread dough. Layer corned beef, sauerkraut, Thousand Island dressing, and cheese. Repeat layers. Bake for 10 to 12 min. Serve with your favorite beer!

Julia Vradelis and Allison Worrell

Stacked Sandwiches

Makes as many as you want

These sandwiches are great for parties or lunch. They work best in the straight muffin tins; however, you can make them any shape and size.

Take the type of bread you want or combine several different kinds for added flavor and colors. These directions are for the smaller straight muffin tins (refer to the "Do You Know the Muffin Pan" section at the beginning of the book).

You will want to cut your bread slices in to circles to fit in to the pan. You can either measure the under side of the muffin cup and trace it on to parchment paper as a guide or find a household cup or glass that is the same size. For our pans, we found that champagne flutes worked great. (Of course, we had to empty them first but it's all in a day's work!)

It usually takes 3 bread circles for each muffin tin, so plan accordingly. Then fill up with your favorite deli meats, cheeses, etc.

Be sure to lightly spray non-stick spray and insert Muffin Pulls so they can be pulled back out or insert a decorative toothpick (after baking) to pull them out.

Filler ideas:

Tuna & Chedder, then top with a dill pickle

Alternate Turkey, Ham, Provolone and Pesto

Try a twist on grilled cheese by adding a layer of sun-dried tomatoes

Slice a Kielbasa thinly and add cheese and spicy brown mustard

Peanut Butter and Jelly or Peanut Butter and Banana

These do not need to be heated long – 5 to 10 minutes at 350 degrees. Be sure to lay them on a paper towel when you remove them so the bottoms don't get soggy.

Make a whole tray of different sandwiches so everyone has a favorite, or let your children help with cutting out the bread, meat and cheese.

Pizza Muffins

Makes as many as you want. (Works best in large muffin cups)

Pizza muffins are fun for everyone to help make and fix with their own toppings! Start with pizza dough, French bread dough, or biscuit dough. Spray muffin cups with non-stick spray. Spread dough in muffin cups – start in the bottom and work the dough up the sides. Sprinkle with garlic salt and oregano. Layer your favorite cheese, meats, veggies, and pizza sauce (2 layers usually fill the cup). Bake at 350° for 10 to 15 min. Remove from oven, lift out of muffin tin, and place a final topping for color!

Kids will love designing their very own pizzas!

Julia Vradelis and Allison Worrell

The Flamin' Ham and Cheese Muffin Meals

Makes 12 regular Muffin Meals

1/4 lb deli sliced honey ham
2 cans crescent roll dough
1 package cubed cheese (any type)
1/2 cup of brown sugar
1 T butter

Preheat the oven for temperature recommended for crescent rolls. Spray muffin pan with non-stick spray. Sauté deli ham in a pan with brown sugar and butter. Roll out crescent dough but do not tear along the perforations. Cut lengthwise along dough to make strips instead of triangles. Place the ham along the dough. Scatter with cubed cheese. Roll up the dough like rolling up a sleeping bag. Pinch one end of the muffin together. Put that end down in the muffin cups.

Bake according to directions for the crescent rolls or until golden brown and flakey. Serve with your favorite condiments such as spicy mustard. Obviously, other meat choices may be substituted. This is also great without meat or with some fresh veggies added.

Sloppy Joe Muffins

Makes 8 large Muffin Meals

1 lb. lean ground beef
1 20 oz. Sweet Baby Ray's Honey BBQ sauce
1 can biscuits (8)
2 cups sharp shredded cheese

Easy. Easy! Easy!!! But always a hit.

Preheat oven to 350 degrees. Spray with non-stick cooking spray. Brown and drain ground beef. Return to the pan. Add BBQ sauce and simmer 10 minutes on low heat. Place each biscuit in muffin cups and press up the edges to form a shell. Fill with beef mixture. Sprinkle a mound of shredded cheese on top. Bake for 15 to 20 minutes or until biscuit is golden brown.

Make this fun as a Halloween Meal. (See "Holiday" section).

This one came from Julia's mom, Vera. You could say this one simple recipe inspired the entire concept of our Muffin Meals.

"She was so wild that when she made French toast she got her tongue caught in the toaster."

--Rodney Dangerfield

Breakfast Muffin
Meals

French Toast Muffins

Makes 6 large Muffin Meals

1 loaf of Texas toast
2 eggs beaten with one T. milk (or 1/2 cup of egg beaters)
Cinnamon
8 ozs cream cheese softened
1/4 cup of powdered sugar
1 can of apple pie filling

Preheat oven to 350°. Insert Muffin Pulls and spray muffin cups with non-stick cooking spray. Cube the bread. Dip each cube in the egg mixture and place in the muffin cups until half full. Press down firmly. Sprinkle with cinnamon. Combine cream cheese and powdered sugar. Spread 2 tablespoons on top of bread cubes, then add a spoonful of apple pie filling. Fill remainder of cup with another bread layer and sprinkle with cinnamon. Cover pan with foil and bake for 8 to 10 minutes. Take out of oven and let cool for about 10 minutes. Top with whipped cream and enjoy!

No need for syrup with this–unless you have an incredible sweet tooth!

Julia Vradelis and Allison Worrell

Granola and Yogurt Breakfast Parfaits

Makes 12 regular size Muffin Meals

Granola Shell:
1/2 cup margarine or butter, softened
1 egg
1/4 cup honey
1 cup oats
1/2 cup whole bran flakes cereal
1/2 cup chopped almonds
1/2 cup flaked coconut
1/2 tsp. cinnamon
1/2 tsp. salt

Fillings:
Yogurt (any flavor)
Fresh fruit
Jam

Preheat oven to 350 degrees. Insert Muffin Pulls and spray each muffin cup with non-stick cooking spray. Mix first 3 ingredients. Add remaining ingredients. Divide evenly in muffin cups (about ½ full). Take the back of a spoon and press evenly and up the sides of the cup to form a "shell". (If it sticks to the spoon, simply spray non-stick cooking spray on spoon). Make foil balls to insert in each cup. Spray with cooking spray before inserting. Bake 10-12 minutes. Let cool down before removing from pan. Fill each shell with your favorite yogurt and fruit and jam. Yummy!

These can also make great bite size treats by making them in your mini muffin tins. Great for brunch finger foods!

Julia Vradelis and Allison Worrell

Hash-browns and Scrambled Egg Muffins

Makes 6 large Muffin Meals

1 bag of refrigerated hash browns
6 eggs, scrambled (not cooked)
1/2 cup each, diced red and green bell peppers
1/4 cup diced onion
2 cups shredded cheddar cheese
Salt and pepper to taste

Preheat oven to 400°. Insert Muffin Pulls into muffin cups and heat pan for 5 min. in the oven. Meanwhile, mix 2 cups of hash browns and 1 cup of cheese. Add 1 teaspoon of salt and 1/2 teaspoon pepper. After pan is heated up remove from oven and spray with non-stick cooking spray. Put enough of the mixture in each muffin cup to cover sides and bottom (use the back of a spoon to press down). Try to move quickly so the pan stays hot. Bake for 10 min. While the hash brown cups are baking, combined the eggs, peppers, onions, and remaining cheese. Put mixture into cooked hash brown cups and cook for 20 to 30 min. or until egg mixture is set.

Julia Vradelis and Allison Worrell

Huevos Rancheros Breakfast Muffins

Makes 6 large Muffin Meals

8 large eggs
1 cup shredded cheddar cheese
6 corn tortillas
1 taco seasoning packet
1/2 cup green onions diced
1/2 cup green peppers diced

1/2 cup red peppers diced
1/2 cup refried beans
Toppings: Shredded cheddar cheese, black olives,
   sour cream, jalapeño slices, guacamole
You will also need tin foil

Preheat oven to 400 degrees. Spray muffin cups with non-stick cooking spray. Insert corn tortilla "pleating" it to fit in muffin cup. Refer to "How-to" section in. Bake 5-10 minutes or until tortillas are lightly browned and crispy. Remove from oven and remove foil balls. Add about 1-2 T. refried beans in each shell and bake an additional 1-2 minutes.

While tortilla shells are baking, crack eggs in a bowl and whisk. Add taco seasoning packet, peppers and onions, and cheese. Pour into hot skillet and stir continuously until eggs are scrambled. Remove tortilla shells from oven and fill with scrambled egg mixture. Remove from pans and top with more cheese, guacamole, sour cream, black olives or jalapeño slices. Feel free to add more spice or tone it down as necessary. These are great served with fresh fruit to cut some of the heat, or, as a friend once told me, "a screwdriver is enough fruit for me."

Hungry Man's Special

Individual recipe (Use large muffin tins)

2 strips uncooked bacon
1/2 cup uncooked hash brown potatoes
1 slice American cheese
1 egg
Salt and Pepper

Preheat oven to 375 degrees. Place Muffin Pulls in large muffin tins and spray with non-stick cooking spray. Place 2 strips of bacon around the muffin cup (when you remove these muffins the bacon will be the sides of the muffin). Put hash browns in muffin cup. With a spoon, press the center down to form a "cup". Take 1/4 square of the slice of cheese and put on top of hash browns. Crack the egg and put the raw egg in the center. If you want these "sunny-side up" don't crack the yolk. Salt and pepper. Bake for 10-15 minutes or until egg is cooked. Great hearty start to your day!

Remember to break the yolk if you don't like it runny!

Julia Vradelis and Allison Worrell

Serve with a side of fresh fruit and you are ready for the day!

Jeweled Fruit Tarts

Filling for 5 Muffin Pies

1 cup sliced strawberries
1 cup sliced bananas
1 cup blackberries or blueberries
Muffin Pie Crusts (see how-to section)

(You can substitute other fruits such as peach slices, kiwi, grapes, etc.)

Glaze:
1/4 cup sugar
1 T. cornstarch
1/3 cup orange juice or pineapple juice
3 T. water
Dash of salt

Mix all the ingredients for the glaze and cook over medium heat until boiling. Stir constantly. Continue to boil and stir for 1 minute until sauce thickens. Remove from heat and cool thoroughly.

Fold fruit in to glaze mixture and fill Muffin Pie Crusts. (See recipe in the "How To" section of this cookbook.)

Julia Vradelis and Allison Worrell

Pancakes and Sausage Muffins

Amount varies
Regular size muffin tins

Pancake mix (can you make pancakes from scratch?) (No, seriously, we don't know)
Ground Sausage, cooked and drained
Ummm. Yep. That's about it.

Preheat oven to 350 degrees. Spray regular sized muffin tins with non-stick cooking spray. Make pancake batter according to directions. Keep in mind that it takes double the batter for each muffin. (i.e. If the recipe says it will make 10-12 pancakes, it will only make 5 muffins.) Fill the muffin tin 2/3 full with pancake batter. Layer with 1 T. cooked sausage. Top with batter to cover sausage completely. Bake for 12-15 minutes. Remove from pan and cover with syrup. Or, if you promise to do another workout that day, you may have a dollup of butter.

So yummy!

Creative touch: Serve this on a "bacon placemat". Yes we know it's extra calories, but splurge every once in a while! To make, just cut 3 long pieces of bacon (the precooked kind) in half to make a total of 6 pieces. Then weave those pieces as you would a basket weave. Carefully place between paper towels and microwave for 45 seconds. That's enough for one placemat.

Sausage Pinwheels

Amount varies

1 cup (about 1/2 roll) of ground pork sausage
1 roll of crescent rolls (you can experiment with this, if you like more bread,
    use pizza dough. If you like less, try pie crust dough)
1/2 cup shredded cheddar cheese
Optional: yellow mustard or honey mustard

Preheat oven to 350 degrees. Place Muffin Pulls in regular sized muffin tins and spray with non-stick cooking spray. Lay out dough on a floured surface or parchment paper. If your using crescent dough, you will need to piece the dough back together where it is perforated. If you like mustard, spread evenly over dough. If not, leave it out. Take a knife and gently spread sausage (small amounts at a time) covering the dough. It will not be completely covered but you get the gist. Is "gist" a word? Anyway, spread cheese on top. Roll it up from the longer side so it's not as bulky. Now slice very thin and place in cups. Depending on how thin you slice these, you may have enough for two trays. Bake for 10-15 minutes or until sausage is completely browned. Remove and drain on paper towels if needed.

These are great alone for brunches or a great side dish, with eggs, for breakfast.

Julia Vradelis and Allison Worrell

Bacon and Eggs Cinnamon Jinx Rolls

Makes 8 regular Muffin Meals

1 can cinnamon rolls
4 eggs beaten
1 box fully cooked bacon

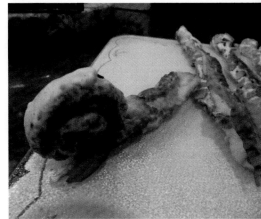

Preheat oven to temperature recommended for cinnamon rolls. Spray muffin pan with non-stick cooking spray. Remove cinnamon rolls from the can. Use a knife to aid in unrolling the cinnamon rolls into strips. Place one piece of bacon on each strip.

Place the roll in muffin pan. Pour beaten eggs over muffins to cover the muffins.

Bake in accordance with instructions for cinnamon rolls. Careful not to overcook. Cool in pan for 5 minutes. Remove from the pan. Top with icing for cinnamons rolls, your favorite jelly, or even syrup.

Julia Vradelis and Allison Worrell

"Seize the moment. Remember all those women on the Titanic who waved off the dessert cart."

--Erma Bombeck

Dessert Muffin
Meals

Banana Nutella Muffins

"Mix to Muffin Cup"

Makes 12 regular Muffin Meals

This dessert is so easy and so scrumptious, you're gonna kick yourself for not thinking of it yourself! But you didn't so here it is in our recipe book...

1 package of Banana Muffin Mix (and ingredients as indicated)
Sliced Bananas (duh)
Nutella (again, duh)
Macadamia Nuts (you might not have seen that coming)
Whipped Cream

Make the banana bread according to directions. Pour into regular sized muffin pans and bake according to directions. Cool completely. Remove from muffin pans. These can be made as tiny bite size desserts or in a regular size muffin pan. Slice each muffin in half. Spread about 2 T. Nutella (1 T. for mini muffins) on bottom half. Layer slices of bananas. Replace top of muffin. Top with whipped cream, chopped macadamia nuts, and a slice of banana.

These would be so cute served at a brunch or luncheon! Yummy!

Julia Vradelis and Allison Worrell

Banana Puddin' Muffin Tart

Makes 12 regular Muffin Meals

8 oz. sour cream
Medium tub Cool Whip
1 small box instant vanilla pudding (make according to directions)
1 box Vanilla Wafers
1 Redi-Whip spray can
1 banana
1 package dried bananas
1/2 stick of butter, melted
1 egg

Preheat oven to 350 degrees. Place Muffin Pulls in muffin cups and spray with non-stick cooking spray. In a medium bowl, crush vanilla wafers. Add butter and eggs. Take 1/4 cup of mixture and press in to cups to form a shell. Bake for 10 minutes. Remove from oven and let cool.

Prepare pudding according to directions on package. Mix with sour cream and Cool Whip. Slice banana and place 3 or 4 slices in the bottom of cups. Fill cups with pudding mixture and refrigerate for at least 30 minutes.

When ready to serve, top with whipped cream and a dried banana chip.

Julia Vradelis and Allison Worrell

Bread Pudding Muffin Cups

Makes 16 large Muffin Meals

18 slices white bread
2 T. margarine or butter
1/2 cup brown sugar
1 tsp. cinnamon
1/2 cup raisins

3 eggs, beaten
1 cup milk
3 T. sugar
1 T. vanilla

Preheat oven to 350 degrees. Insert Muffin Pulls in large muffin cups. Spray with non-stick cooking spray. Toast bread slices very lightly. (Do not brown.) Spread each slice with butter and sprinkle with brown sugar and cinnamon. Cut into cubes. Fill each muffin cup with 3 slices of bread (already cubed). Push the bread down in to the cup to stick together. Fill all six cups. Combine eggs, milk, sugar, and vanilla. Pour about ¼ cup of mixture over each bread pudding cup. Bake 20 minutes.

While pudding is baking, mix up the Bourbon Sauce.

1/2 cup butter
1 cup sugar
1 egg, beaten
1/4 cup bourbon (whiskey)

Melt butter in a saucepan over low heat. Add sugar and whisk in egg, stirring constantly. Continue to heat until sauce thickens slightly. Cool for about 5 minutes. Add bourbon, stir. Reheat before pouring on pudding cups.

You will feel like you've died and gone to New Orleans!

Julia Vradelis and Allison Worrell

Caramel Apple Muffins

Makes 12 regular Muffin Meals

6 red apples
2 rolls pie pastry dough
1 tub Litehouse caramel dip

Preheat oven to 350 degrees. Insert Muffin Pulls into muffin cups and spray with non-stick cooking spray. Roll out pie dough on wax paper. With pizza cutter, cut in 4 to 5 equal strips. Then cut in half in the opposite direction. This will yield 8-10 pieces. Place 1 square of pie dough in each cup. Next place another piece of dough at an angle to the first piece.

Dice apples and place in a bowl. Mix with enough caramel dip to generously coat apple pieces. Spoon filling into each cup to the top. Fold edges of pie dough over top and stretch to pinch the edges. Bake 10-15 minutes until the crust is golden brown. Cool until Muffin Pulls can lift the muffins out. Place on serving plate and drizzle with the caramel dip. The dip may need to be warmed slightly to drizzle. Garnish with apple wedges. May use green apple or a mixture for a more tart muffin.

Julia Vradelis and Allison Worrell

Chocolate Chip Cookie Muffin Cups

You can use any size muffin pan for these so amounts will vary

When I was in 8th grade Home Economics class, my teacher had us make bacon crackers. You take a piece of bacon and wrap it around a saltine cracker and broil it. She made us write that "recipe" down. I though, "How absurd. Who wouldn't remember this ridiculous recipe?" That's kind of how I feel about this recipe but here it is anyway…

1 roll of cookie dough (any kind)
Ice cream (your favorite flavor)
Toppings – chocolate syrup, Whipped topping, maraschino cherries, crushed nuts, sprinkles (you get the picture)

Preheat oven to 350 degrees. Place one muffin pull in each cup. (One is all you need.) Spray muffin tins (any size – your call) with non-stick cooking spray. Press cookie dough in tins to make a "cup". Place a foil ball (also sprayed with cooking spray) in each cup to maintain the shape and bake. Medium cups – 10-12 min. Mini cups – 5-7 min.

Let the cookie cups cool completely. Remove and fill with your favorite ice cream and toppings.

Should we go over this again?

Julia Vradelis and Allison Worrell

Dottie's Strawberry Cake Muffins

Makes 12 regular Muffin Meals

Muffin ingredients:
1 box white cake mix
1 small box strawberry jello
4 eggs
1 cup frozen strawberries in syrup
3/4 cup cooking oil
1/4 cup water
(if using fresh strawberries, use ½ cup of water instead)

Frosting ingredients:
1 cup fresh or frozen strawberries (no syrup)
1 box confectionary sugar
1 stick softened butter

Preheat oven to 350 degrees. Spray muffin cups with non-stick cooking spray. Mix all muffin ingredients together for 2 minutes. Pour in muffin pan. Bake for 25-30 minutes. Test with a toothpick so that it comes out clean. Follow cake box instructions for cooling and remove from the pan. To prepare frosting, mix all ingredients and beat until smooth. May substitute cream cheese for butter for creamier frosting. Frost muffins when cool. For more moist muffins, drizzle with strawberry syrup from frozen berries before frosting. Garnish with fresh strawberries or even other fresh berries such as raspberries and blueberries.

Allison has fond memories of her mother, Dottie making this for her brother every birthday. Make this for someone special!

Julia Vradelis and Allison Worrell

Pineapple Upside Down Luau Muffins

Makes 12 regular Muffin Meals

1 can chunk pineapple drained
1/2 can crushed pineapple drained
1 box Ritz crackers
1 stick softened butter

2 cups sharp cheddar cheese
1/2 cup of sugar
1 can Redi Whip spray
Kiwi (optional)

Preheat oven to 350 degrees. Insert Muffin Pulls and spray with non-stick cooking spray. Crush Ritz crackers and combine with 1 stick of butter. Mold and press crust mixture firmly into the bottom 1/3 of each cup. In a mixing bowl, combine the chunk pineapple, the crushed pineapple, the shredded cheese, and the sugar and stir. Spoon the mixture into each cup and fill to the top. Bake at 350 degrees for 20-30 minutes or until bubbling and tops begin to turn golden. Cool for 10-15 minutes and remove from the pan with the Muffin Pulls. Garnish with Redi Whip cool whip and serve warm. For the real cheese lover sprinkle with more shredded cheese.

There are many additions that would make this muffin even more tasty. Try adding other fruits like Kiwi to the pineapple or as a garnish.

Diana O'Brien Whaley, contributor

Tiramisu Muffin Cups

Makes 6 large Muffin Meals

This is a bit of a twist on an old favorite

Shells:
3 cups crushed ladyfinger cookies (with icing between)
6 T. coffee liquor
1/2 cup of melted chocolate chips

Filling:
3 cups prepared vanilla pudding
1 cup sour cream
1 T. coffee liquor
Cinnamon, Whipped topping, and extra
 cookies for garnish

Combine finely crushed cookies and coffee liquor. (You can crush the cookies in a food processor or simply use a good old potato masher, but remember to include the frosting.) Put Muffin Pulls in large muffin cups and spray with non-stick cooking spray. Put ½ cup of cookie mixture in to each cup and press into the bottom of cup and up the sides to form a "shell". Put about 1 T. of melted chocolate in each cup and spread the chocolate up the sides so it is "lined" with chocolate. Put muffin pan in refrigerator for 30 minutes to harden the chocolate.

While the shells are chilling, combine vanilla pudding, sour cream, and coffee liquor.

Remove shells from the refrigerator and fill with pudding mixture. Top with whipped cream and press a cookie (separate the two sides and use the plain side – no frosting). Sprinkle with cinnamon and enjoy!

"If you really want to make a friend, go to someone's house and eat with him...the people who give you their food give you their heart."

--Cesar Chavez

Holiday Muffin *Meals*

Valentine's Chocolate Covered Cherry Muffins

"Mix to Muffin Cup"

Makes 12 large Muffins

1 White Cake mix with ingredients
2 cups mini chocolate chips
1 small box jello (black cherry or cherry)
Can of whipped topping
Red sugar for decoration
Chocolate syrup

Preheat oven to 350 degrees. Insert Muffin Pulls in to large muffin tins and spray with non-stick cooking spray. Mix cake batter according to directions. Add chocolate chips and bake. (Add a few extra minutes than what is indicated for smaller muffin cups.) Cupcakes are done when you insert a toothpick and it comes out clean. Remove from oven and let cool.

While muffins are cooling, make chocolate drizzle hearts for topping. You will need 1 cup of chocolate chips (this is in addition to the 2 cups added to the batter). Put the chips in a sandwich bag and microwave for 20-30 seconds or until melted. (This can also be done over the stove then spooned in to baggies). Snip the corner off of one end of the bag and pipe hearts on wax or parchment paper on a plate or tray. You'll find the pattern for the heart in the "How-to" section to use as a guide. After you have made your hearts, place them in the refrigerator or freezer to harden.

Julia Vradelis and Allison Worrell

Next, prepare the jello as directed but do not put in the refrigerator as instructed. When muffins are cool, remove from muffin tins and put them on a plate or tray. Take a small dowel rod or lollipop stick, and poke holes in each one. Drizzle a good amount of the liquid jello in each muffin. Refrigerate for 1 hour.

When ready to serve, drizzle each muffin with chocolate sauce, top with whipped topping, sprinkle with red sugar. Finally add your beautiful lacy chocolate heart. You'll fall in love!

Each drizzle heart should be about 1 to 2" in diameter

Shown without chocolate syrup. Just as yummy!

Irish Beef and Cabbage Cups

Makes 6 regular sized Muffin Meals

1 cup (2 to 3 – 2oz. packages) of chipped beef or sliced corned beef* chopped
1 cup cabbage chopped
1 cup carrots chopped
1/2 cup parsley chopped
8oz. carton of sour cream
1/2 cup Miracle Whip
1 pkg. of dry vegetable soup mix
1 roll of refrigerated pizza dough (we used whole wheat for this recipe)

Preheat oven to 350 degrees. Spray regular sized muffin cups with non-stick cooking spray. Roll out pizza dough to roughly 18" x 12" rectangle. Cut out Clover shapes either free hand or using the top of a heart shaped cookie cutter. Leave the base together as shown.

Carefully place clover shapes into muffin cups and press down the bottom and sides leaving the edges of the clovers coming out of the cups.

Julia Vradelis and Allison Worrell

Because these overlap, you may need to use 2 pans to make 6 muffins.

Meanwhile, combine all remaining ingredients and divide among the clover shells. Bake for 10-15 minutes until filling is bubbling and crust is golden brown. Top with chopped parsely and serve with a hearty beer and an Irish toast!

Time saver – Instead of buying an entire head of cabbage, pick up a package of cole slaw found in the bagged salads area of the grocery store.

*We used the Budding brand sliced beef found with luncheon meats.

(If you are ambitious enough to cook a corned beef for hours, our little leprechaun hats are off to ya!)

Easter Basket Muffins

Makes 6 large baskets

This is a great way to serve your leftover Easter ham or hard-boiled eggs in a festive bread basket!

Start with the basic "Bread Basket" recipe in the "How To" section.

Bake the "handles" on a separate cookie sheet. You can bake them together with your baskets, but they require much less time. Bake baskets on the upper shelf for about 10 min. or until golden. The handles only take about 5 min. Let your baskets cool. Line with lettuce and fill with egg or ham salad made from your Easter leftovers.

Julia Vradelis and Allison Worrell

Freedom Franks and Bean Muffins

Makes 6 large Muffin Meals

This is a twist on the typical hot dog, baked beans, and coleslaw everyone serves on the 4th of July.

3 hot dog buns cut into about 1/2 inch cubes
3 hot dogs cut into small slices
1 egg beaten

Onion powder
1 can of your favorite baked beans
2 cups prepared coleslaw

Preheat oven to 350 degrees. Insert Muffin Pulls in to large muffin cups and spray with non-stick cooking spray. Take each bread cube, dip in egg and place in to muffin cup. (Do not saturate, just lightly dip). Fill the cup with bread cubes, forming a shell. Press together with the back of a spoon or with your hands to form a cup. (It should be about ¾ inch thick on the bottom and about ½ inch around the sides.) Sprinkle with onion powder.

Combine beans and hot dogs and fill each cup with mixture. Bake for 10-15 minutes. Let stand for about 5 minutes then remove from muffin pan.

Top with coleslaw and serve!

Creative touch: Wrap these with festive red, white, and blue paper wrappers you can make by tracing the pattern in the back of the book. Remember to line the regular paper with a wrapper of parchment paper or wax paper otherwise it will bleed through regular scrapbook paper.

Julia Vradelis and Allison Worrell

Fall Leaf Pies

Start with the original Chicken Pot Pie recipe under the "Chicken" section.

The individual pot pies make a delicious gift. Add a festive bow for an additional touch!

Use colorful scrapbook paper to line the pan

Simply cut the leaf out of pastry dough and brush with egg whites before baking.

Julia Vradelis and Allison Worrell

Jack-O-Sloppy Joe

These are so easy but so fun for a Halloween party or to have available after trick-or-treating!

Simply start with the Sloppy Joe muffin recipe and bake. While the sloppy Joe's are baking, take individual cheese slices (we use Kraft singles) and cut out pumpkin heads and faces. We recommend laying these on wax paper so you can peel them off easily.

Kids can help make their own faces so they are all different. After the sloppy Joe's come out of the oven, carefully lay your pumpkin faces on each sloppy Joe. Use a bay leaf or a piece of green pepper for the stem. No need for additional baking, the cheese will melt perfectly!

Tom Turkey Muffins

Amounts vary- Large Muffin Pan works best

Stuffing (already cooked)
Turkey (already cooked)
Jellied cranberry sauce
Red, green, orange, and yellow peppers
Cream cheese
Peppercorns

Preheat oven to 350°. Insert Muffin Pulls and spray with non-stick cooking spray. Fill each muffin cup 1/2 full with prepared, cooked stuffing. Add a layer of 2 tablespoons jellied cranberry sauce. Fill the remainder of the cup with cooked shredded turkey. Bake for 10 min. (note: if using leftovers you may want to add a little chicken broth or water to stuffing and turkey to keep it moist). Meanwhile, cut peppers into strips. After the muffins are done, let sit for about 5 min. before removing. Insert toothpicks into peppers. Add cream cheese and peppercorns to the red pepper strip to make the turkey's eyes. Insert the yellow, green, and orange peppers to make the feathers. This is a great idea for your kids to gobble up any leftovers!

Julia Vradelis and Allison Worrell

Christmas Cocoa Cups

"Mix to Muffin Cup"

Makes 24 regular sized Muffin Desserts

1 Chocolate Cupcake mix (with ingredients to make)
1 bag of malted milk balls
1 jar Marshmallow fluff
1 jar vanilla icing

1 bag large marshmallows
Green sugar
Cinnamon candies

Preheat oven according to cupcake mix instructions. Spray two 12-muffin pans with non-stick cooking spray. Pour batter in to cups about 1/3 full. Place one of the malted milk balls in each muffin cup then cover with batter until 2/3 full.

Bake according to mix directions. While the muffins are baking, cut each marshmallow into thirds. Then trim the sides of each piece to look like a holly leaf and dip into green sugar to coat one side. These get so sticky you are going to want to say a bad word. But don't. It is the Christmas season after all. You will need 3 for each muffin so pull up a chair and put on some music.

When muffins are done baking, remove from pan and let cool thoroughly.

Combine vanilla icing and marshmallow fluff. Frost cooled muffins with marshmallow fluff mixture and finish with three holly leaves and 3 cinnamon candies for the berries.

Julia Vradelis and Allison Worrell

How-To's

Muffin Pie Shells
(each 9" pie crust makes 5 regular muffin cup pie shells)

Prepared refrigerated Pie Crust

You will use these for the Jeweled Fruit recipe in the "Breakfast" section or the Chicken Pot Pie Muffins in the "Chicken" section. Feel free to use this "shell" for other fillings.

Preheat oven to 350 degrees. Spray regular muffin pans with non-stick cooking spray. Unroll either one or both pie crusts depending on how many muffin pie shells you want. These will freeze so make as many as you want! Typically it is best to unroll the dough on a floured surface or parchment paper. Now simply cut out circles with a diameter of 4 3/4 to 5". Use a bowl or saucer of these dimensions; or, we found a margarita glass is the perfect size! You should be able to cut out 4 circles from a 9" pie crust, then reroll the scraps for the 5th circle.

Note: If you are making the crusts for the Chicken Pot Pie Muffins, you will need to make your circles 5 1/2 to 6" in diameter because that recipe is made in the large muffin pans. Obviously, to make 6, you will need 2 of the 9" pie crusts.

Place each dough circle in a muffin cup. They will be slightly pleated. If you like that look, simply leave as is. If you want to make a traditional crimped pie crust edge, flatten out the pleats inside the cup, fold over the top edge, and either crimp with your fingers or pierce with a fork all the way around. You may want to stagger these in the cups as they hang over the edges a bit. (See photo showing both types.) Pierce the bottom of cups with a fork so the dough doesn't puff up during baking. If you would like the edges to "shine", brush with egg whites before baking.

Bake for 15 minutes or until golden brown. Let cool completely. Fill with your favorite filling or freeze until ready to use later!

Rice or Stuffing Cups

3 cups cooked rice or stuffing mix (whatever the Muffin recipe calls for)

In preparing the rice cups (or shells) for several recipes, the key is to cook the rice then let it set for at least 10-15 minutes. Normally we want our rice light and fluffy, but in making the cups for these recipes, you actually want it a bit sticky. You can even add a bit of cheese (if it makes sense for that recipe) to help it stick together better. You also want to really smash it together with your fingers or the back of a spoon.

Julia Vradelis and Allison Worrell

Another hint is to leave it in the pan for at least 10 minutes. Don't be in a rush to take it out of the pan. They are more likely to fall apart. These shell are used in the "Good Old Chicken and Rice" and "Caribbean Shrimp" Muffins.

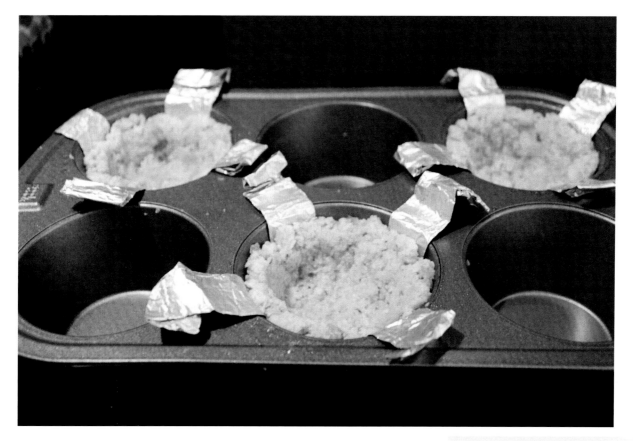

Tortilla Cups

You know how you run out of paper coffee filters and you take a paper towel and kind of fold it to make it fit? That's how you make the tortilla cups. Just remember to spray it with non-stick cooking spray and lightly salt for flavor before cooking. You will bake these at 400 degrees for about 10 minutes or until slightly crispy.

This shell was used in the Chicken Fajita, Chicken Enchiladas, Mexican Chicken and Corn, and Huevos Rancheros.

Julia Vradelis and Allison Worrell

Phyllo Cups

You will use these in the Chicken and Spinach Dip Muffins under the "Chicken" section.

Insert Muffin Pulls in muffin cups and spray with non-stick cooking spray. Spread out refrigerated Phyllo dough (or thawed out frozen dough) on parchment paper. Cut in to 6 squares. Separate each layer and place in muffin cups and spray each layer lightly with cooking spray. Try to "stagger" each layer so it is not lined up. This will give it an almost "blossom-like" appearance.

This recipe in the book, calls for you to fill these cups prior to baking. If you use these in other recipes, be aware that these cook rather quickly – 10 to 12 minutes!

Woven Bread Baskets

Makes 6 large baskets

2 cans refrigerated thin crust Pizza dough
1 egg white

Preheat oven to 350 degrees

Turn over your large muffin tin and spray thoroughly with non-stick cooking spray.

Spread out pizza dough on non-stick surface or parchment paper. Cut out 12 circles to make the bottom of the basket. Use one of your glasses or cups that is about the same size as the bottom of your large muffin cups. Place one of the dough circles on each muffin cup. See photo:

Cut the remaining dough into strips. For each cup you will need 12 2-inch strips and 3 strips 8-inches long.

Take the smaller strips and arrange them around the dough circle pressing all 12 strips in to the dough to make them stay. they will stretch out a bit during the weaving but you can trim them after. Now place the other cut out circle on top to secure the smaller strips.

Take the longer strip and begin at the top (which is actually the bottom) and weave it over and under each smaller strip. Do the same, but opposite over under, for the additional 2 rows.

Now simply trip any excess from the bottom and gently press together to eliminate any holes.

Before baking be sure to brush with egg whites. This will give the baskets a pretty "shine".

Bake for 10-15 minutes or until golden brown. These can be frozen for later use. Great for soups or stews or even salads as shown in the holiday section.

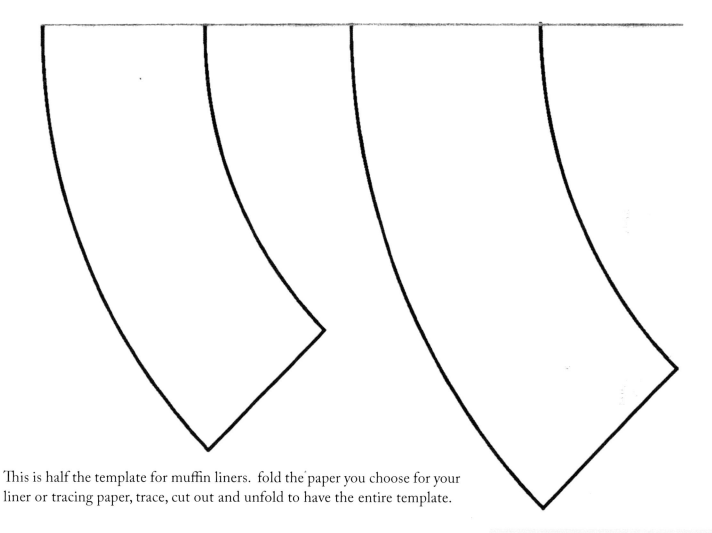

This is half the template for muffin liners. fold the paper you choose for your liner or tracing paper, trace, cut out and unfold to have the entire template.

Julia Vradelis and Allison Worrell

Copyright Acknowledgements

Allegro Original Marinade

Sweet Baby Ray's

Zatarains

Miracle Whip

Knorr's Soup Mix

Kraft Macaroni and Cheese

Budding Corn Beef slices

Kraft Cheese Singles

Cool Whip

Litehouse Caramel

Nutella

Redi Whip

Ritz Crackers

And Last But Not Least…Bloopers

We had so many laughs (and tears) during this process that we thought we should share some of them with you. So here are a few of the things that are said when two old friends get together to cook and write.

When we came up with the idea of writing this book, the reaction from our kids was very mixed. No it wasn't, come to think of it.

Hali (Julia's daughter): "Wait. You're writing a cookbook? You? And Miss Allison? And You????"
Jordan (Allison's daughter): "Why are the two mom's who never cook writing a cookbook? I don't get it."
Sophie (Julia's daughter): "But you don't cook. And I don't think you write."
Lindsey (Allison's daughter): "I don't think this is a good idea. I really don't"

We both like Mexican food so one of our first recipes was the Chicken Enchilada Muffin. We probably eat Mexican food once a week. So this seemed like a great place to start. Here is how it went.

Julia: "What's in a Chicken Enchilada?"
Allison: "I have no idea."

.

Upon taking one of our recipes out of the oven:

Allison: "Well that's just a hot mess!"
Julia: "Maybe we could make "Hot Mess" one of our sections."
Allison: "It would be a huge section."

At one of our planning sessions:

Julia: "We can just roll it out on parchment paper."
Allison: Nodding her head. "Yeah that's a good idea."
Julia: "You know, because nothing sticks to it."
Allison: Nodding her head enthusiastically…
(Awkward silence)
Allison: "I don't know what parchment paper is."

And finally, at the end of the day:

Allison and Julia: "We really can cook. Just don't tell our families!"